Group's Singable Songs for Children's Ministry

ACCOMPANIMENT & LEADERS GUIDE

COMPANION PRODUCTS:

Lyrics Big Book for Group Singing

Lyrics Big Book for More Group Singing

Split-Channel Cassette, Volumes 1–4

Split-Channel Compact Disc, Volumes 1–4

Loveland, Colorado

GROUP'S SINGABLE SONGS FOR CHILDREN'S MINISTRY: ACCOMPANIMENT & LEADERS GUIDE

CREDITS

Songbook Team: Jody Brolsma, Lisa Chandler, Pam Clifford, Jim Kellett, Brenda Kraft, Susan Lingo, Virginia Myers, Kerri Nance, Mike Nappa, Steve Saavedra, Joani Schultz, and Jennifer Root Wilger
Songbook Team Coordinators: Mike Nappa and Pam Clifford
Music Arranger: Jonathan B. Heely
Music Engraver: A-R Editions
Creative Products Director: Joani Schultz
Editors: Mike Nappa and Pam Clifford
Copy Editor: Janis Sampson
Editorial Assistant: Kerri Nance
Art Director: Lisa Chandler
Cover Art Director: Liz Howe
Cover Designer: Randy Miller
Cover Photographer: Craig DeMartino
Computer Graphic Artist: Rosalie Lawrence
Illustrators: Joan Holub and Rebecca McKillip Thornburgh
Audio Engineer: Steve Saavedra
Production Manager: Gingar Kunkel
Sign Language Consultant: Virginia Myers

ISBN 1-55945-464-4
10 9 8 7 6 5 4 3 2 1   05 04 03 02 01 00 99 98 97 96
Printed in the United States of America.

Contents

Introduction

Welcome to the All-in-One Music Resource for Children's Ministry!

What you hold in your hands is not just another kids' songbook—it's an innovative and practical new tool for music ministry. Here's what you'll find in the pages of *Group's Singable Songs for Children's Ministry: Accompaniment & Leaders Guide*.

- A wide variety of children's songs—62 in all! These include classics such as "The Wise Man and the Foolish Man" and "The Butterfly Song," contemporary hits such as "The Holy Books" by James Ward and "Hip, Hip, Hooray" by Mary Rice Hopkins, and brand-new releases such as "Sing If You Wanna Be Happy" by Caye Cook and "The Family" by Barry McGuire and Mark Royce.
- A wide variety of musical styles including rap, country, reggae, pop, traditional, and more.
- Piano accompaniment and guitar chords for each song.
- Action ideas and sign language for many of the songs.
- Easy-to-use indexes listing titles, themes, scriptural tie-ins, energy levels, sign language songs, and action songs.
- Songs by well-known Christian musicians such as Mary Rice Hopkins, Barry McGuire, James Ward, Bill and Gloria Gaither, and others.
- Songs that children's ministry workers across America requested—and that you'll want to lead.

So Now That I've Got It, What Do I Do With It?

Thought you'd never ask! The answer is simple: Use it!

If you're a Sunday school teacher, a children's church worker, a children's worship leader, a children's choir director, a VBS volunteer, a midweek meeting leader, a parent, a day-care provider, or someone who simply enjoys music and children, then *Group's Singable Songs for Children's Ministry: Accompaniment & Leaders Guide* is for you.

As a result of using this product, you'll
- have a wide variety of songs to use for leading children in singing,
- be armed with extra tools, such as action ideas and sign language instructions, for making a children's sing-along time special,
- be able to put together a meaningful sing-along time quickly and easily (thanks to the comprehensive indexes),
- be able to generate enthusiasm for a children's sing-along time with little prep and expense, and
- feel more confident in your ability to create an exciting sing-along time for children.

Kids, Join the Band!

Leading kids in singing is just the beginning of the fun. Why not let the children in your group "join the band"? Using one or more of the 10 ideas that follow, show kids how to make inexpensive musical instruments. Then, when it's time to sing, let kids strike up the band!

1. Shake, Rattle, and Roll

Set out cardboard tubes (from empty paper towel or toilet paper rolls), 4-inch squares of wax paper, spoons, uncooked rice, rubber bands, and markers. Allow kids a few moments to decorate the outside of their cardboard tubes with the markers. Then show each student how to cover one end of the tube with a wax paper square, securing the paper by wrapping a rubber band around the tube several times. Next have each child put two spoonfuls of rice into the open end of the tube and then close it off with wax paper and a rubber band. Make sure the rubber bands are on the tubes securely before allowing kids to shake the tubes. Kids can shake, rattle, and roll their tubes to the rhythm of the music!

2. Strum With Your Thumb

Have each child bring in one empty, clean aluminum soda can. Be sure each can has an intact tab. Have half the class fill their soda cans with water. Then show children how to gently "strum" the tab with a thumb to produce a "banjo" sound. Have kids listen for the different sounds of the full and empty cans. Kids can also cup the cans in their hands and then strum the tabs for different sounds.

3. Drumsticks

Collect empty, clean 2-liter soda bottles to use as "drums." Have each student hold two bottles by the necks and bang them together. When struck together, the middle portions of the bottles will give off deep "thump" or "bang" sounds. The more kids use these instruments, the better sound they make. The drumstick sound is a great accompaniment to clapping and stomping in livelier songs.

4. Cancan Castanets

Have children collect the metal lids from frozen juice cans (the kind that are held in place with a plastic strip). You'll need two lids for each child. Help each child hot glue a strip of elastic (any size) to one side of each lid. When the glue has dried, have students place the lids together so the elastic strips are on the top and bottom. Have each child slip two fingers under the top strip and a thumb under the bottom strip. Demonstrate how to clap the castanets together by "clapping" the lids with your thumb and fingers.

5. Two Percent Tom-Toms

Form pairs and give each pair two empty, clean half-gallon milk cartons. Have kids fasten the long sides of these together using tape or glue. Then give each pair a generous handful of paper clips and have them place these inside one of the milk cartons. Help kids staple both of their cartons shut. Kids can use their hands or unsharpened pencils to drum on their "tom-toms." The carton with paper clips inside will sound a bit like a snare drum, while the other carton will sound more like a bongo.

6. Jingle All the Way

Give each student two sturdy paper plates, a sharpened pencil, a 2-foot length of string, scissors, and seven jingle bells. Set markers, crayons, and glue in the middle of the room. Demonstrate how to glue the paper plates together so that the outer rims are touching. (This will leave a hollow space between the plates.)

When the glue has dried, have each student use a pencil to poke seven holes around the edges of their plates. Then show them how to slip the string through a hole and tie on a jingle bell. When each student has attached all seven jingle bells to the plate, the "tambourine" can be shaken or tapped to make different sounds.

Option: You may want to use old keys, available at most thrift stores, instead of jingle bells. Each student can string on two keys loosely at each hole in the plate—the keys will move around and make a jingling sound.

7. Fabulous Foot Banjos

Give a disposable plastic cup, 12 inches of fishing line, and a safety pin to each student. Have each one use the safety pin to make a small hole in the bottom of the cup. Then demonstrate how to poke the fishing line through the hole and tie a knot.

The knot will be on the underside of the cup, as shown in the diagram. Have children sit on the floor with their legs straight out in front of them and then place the rim of the cups against the soles of their shoes. Show them how to pull the fishing line taut (gently) and strum it. Older children may want to make a more advanced "banjo" with three strings. The strings can be "tuned" by altering their lengths.

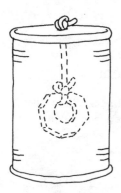

8. Mooosical Bells

Give each student a clean, empty soup can; a hammer; a small nail; a 4-inch length of leather lacing; and a large bolt. Show each student how to use the hammer and nail to make a hole in the center of the bottom of the can. Have kids remove the nails and set them aside. Then have each student tie the bolt securely to one end of the leather lacing, slip the other end through the hole in the can, and knot it. When each student holds the can with the open end down, the bolt will hang down inside the can. Show kids how to shake the cans from side to side and make their cowbells ring!

Option: Younger children can make a simpler version using a paper cup and a jingle bell. Help each child use a toothpick to poke a hole in the bottom of the cup. Then show them how to attach jingle bells to the cups with string.

9. Water Chimes

Gather several glass jars and fill them with water of varying amounts. Give each student one of these jars and have them take turns tapping the jar with a ruler or a pen. Then have kids work together to put their "chimes" in order from the lowest to the highest sound. Kids can put food coloring in the water to make each "note" a different color to help them remember their scale. If you leave the water chimes on a counter or shelf, kids can "chime in" during singing time!

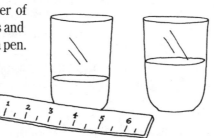

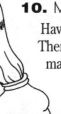

10. Marbleous Maraca Mittens

Have each student fill the toes of two old socks with five or six marbles. Then have students use yarn to tie off the marble area, leaving room for the marbles to move around slightly. Next show children how to put their hands in the socks (like mittens) so the marble "sacks" touch the tips of their fingers. When kids clap their hands, the marble sacks will smack together for a fun sound.

This Is Great—But I Want More!

You want it? You've got it! If you like *Group's Singable Songs for Children's Ministry: Accompaniment & Leaders Guide*, you'll love the companion products that go along with it. Check out these additional resources:
● *Lyrics Big Book for Group Singing*
● *Lyrics Big Book for More Group Singing*
● Split-Channel Cassette, Volumes 1–4
● Split-Channel Compact Disc, Volumes 1–4

Group's Singable Songs for Children's Ministry: Accompaniment & Leaders Guide is too much fun to keep to yourself. Why not try it out with a group of children today? You (and your kids) will be glad you did!

Come, Meet Jesus!

Words and Music by Mary Rice Hopkins

THEME	SCRIPTURE	ENERGY LEVEL
Jesus, our friend	John 15:15	High

best ___ friend. ___ He brought us life in - to this world, ___ his
go. _____ His truth will spread like a plant - ed seed

love and joy _____ have no ___ end.
as our friend - ship grows. _____

D.S. al Coda

sus!

Come, Meet Jesus!

Chorus:
Come a come a come a come a come along.

Come, meet   Jesus!

Come a come a come a come a come on sing this song.

Come, meet   Jesus!

1. I want to introduce you

To my very, very best   friend.

He brought us life into this world,

His love and joy have no end.

(Sing Chorus)
2. Jesus'   love will never leave.

Though   friends   will   come and go.

His truth will spread like a planted seed

As our friendship   grows.

(Sing Chorus)

Lord, I Lift Your Name on High

Words and Music by Rick Founds

THEME	SCRIPTURE	ENERGY LEVEL
Praising God/Jesus, our Savior	Psalm 148:13	Medium

Lord, I lift your name on high;

Lord, I love to sing your prais - es.

I'm so glad you're in my life;

I'm so glad you came to save us.

You came from heav - en to earth to show the way,

from the earth _____ to the cross, ___ my debt _____ to pay. _

From the cross _____ to the grave, ___ from the grave _____ to the sky; _

Lord, I lift your name _ on high! _____

Down in Bethlehem

Words and Music by David Ray Hitt

THEME	SCRIPTURE	ENERGY LEVEL
Christmas/Jesus' birth	Luke 2:1-7	Low

Lyrics under the staves:

1. Some-thing's go - ing on ____
4. Some-thing's go - ing on ____

down in Beth - le - hem. An - gels are a - sing - ing down in Beth - le - hem.
down in Beth - le - hem. An - gels are a - sing - ing down in Beth - le - hem.

And we can see the ba - by gent - ly ly - ing in a man - ger, with the
And you can see ____ Ma - ry gent - ly cry - ing, For her Son will soon be

host of hea - ven cry - ing, ____ "Bless - ing, glo - ry, hon - or, and pow - er to

him." ____

2. Shep-herds are a - shak - ing
3. An - gel told the wise men:

To Coda

Down in Bethlehem

The B-I-B-L-E

Author Unknown

THEME	SCRIPTURE	ENERGY LEVEL
God's Word	2 Timothy 3:16	High

The B - I - B - L - E, yes, that's the Book for me. I stand a-lone on the Word of God. The B - I - B - L - E! The E! The B - I - B - L - E, yes, that's the Book for me. I stand a-lone on the Word of God. The B - I - B - L - E!

ACTIONS for THE B-I-B-L-E

The B-I-B-L-E,

Yes, that's the Book for me.

I stand alone on the Word of God.

The B-I-B-L-E!

(Repeat twice)

SIGN LANGUAGE for THE B-I-B-L-E

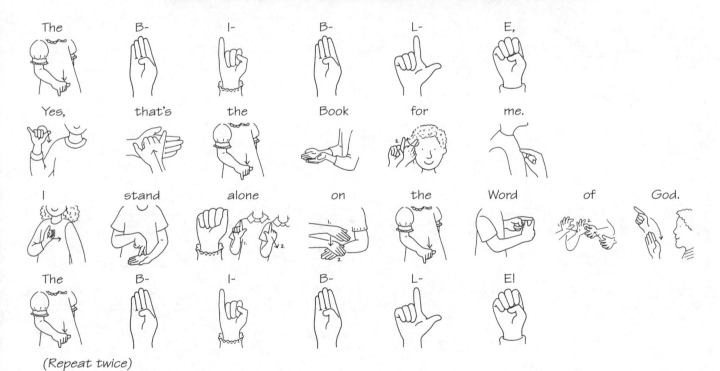

The B- I- B- L- E,

Yes, that's the Book for me.

I stand alone on the Word of God.

The B- I- B- L- E!

(Repeat twice)

1 Thessalonians 4:17

Words and Music by Rusty Wills

THEME
Eternal life/Scripture song

SCRIPTURE
1 Thessalonians 4:17

ENERGY LEVEL
Medium

Awesome God

Words and Music by Rich Mullins

THEME	SCRIPTURE	ENERGY LEVEL
God's power	Psalm 113:4-6	Medium

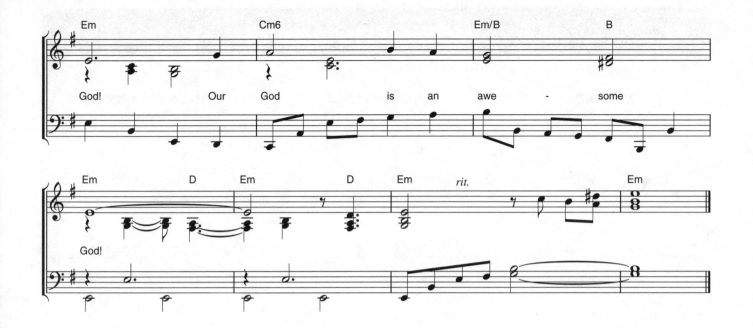

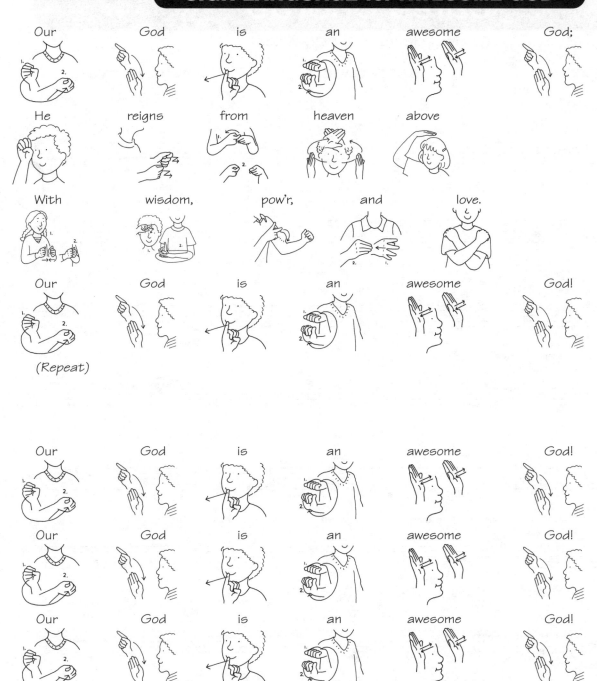

Our   God   is   an   awesome   God;

He   reigns   from   heaven   above

With   wisdom,   pow'r,   and   love.

Our   God   is   an   awesome   God!

(Repeat)

Our   God   is   an   awesome   God!

Our   God   is   an   awesome   God!

Our   God   is   an   awesome   God!

Cares Chorus

Words and Music by Kelly Willard

THEME	SCRIPTURE	ENERGY LEVEL
Trusting God/Scripture song	1 Peter 5:7	Low

cast all of my cares _ up - on you, on you, I will

cast all my cares up - on you.

The Best Gift

Words and Music by Mary Rice Hopkins

THEME	SCRIPTURE	ENERGY LEVEL
Christmas/Jesus' birth	Matthew 1:18-25	Medium

1. Wrapped up in a man-ger ___ a long, long time a-go, ___ God ___ sent ___ his on-ly Son ___ so his love ___ we'd know.

Jesus gave ___ his life ___ so we could be ___ set free, ___ find true ___ for-give - ness, ___ God's

2. Thank you, God, for all the gifts you give us ev-ery day. ___ The sun and moon and stars so bright, ___ and friends a-long ___ the way.

Most of all ___ I thank ___ you for your pre-cious Son ___ who came ___ so I can know ___ and love ___ like him. ___ I'll

The Best Gift

1. Wrapped   up   in a manger

A long, long time ago,

God sent his only Son

So his love we'd know.

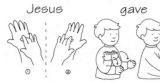

Jesus   gave   his life

So we could be set free,

Find true forgiveness,

God's   gift   to   you   and   me.

Chorus:
The best   gift   to   me, the best   gift   to   me,

His name is   Jesus!

Thank you,   God,   for   Jesus!

The best   gift   to   me.

2. Thank you,   God, for all the   gifts

You   give   us every day.

The sun and moon and stars so bright,

And   friends   along the way.

Most of all I thank you for

Your precious Son who came

So I can know and love like him.

I'll sing about his name.

(Sing Chorus)

The Best Gift

Celebration Song

Words and Music by Mary Rice Hopkins

THEME
Celebration/Joy

SCRIPTURE
Psalm 100

ENERGY LEVEL
Medium

Celebration Song

ACTIONS for CELEBRATION SONG

1. You may not have much rhythm,

You may not play the guitar,

But ev'ryone can celebrate

No matter who you are.

If you have feet, then you can dance.

If you have a voice, then sing.

If you have hands, then reach out

With the love that   Jesus   brings.

Chorus:
  So c'mon, sing along,

  Shake somebody's hand.

Let's celebrate what God has done

With his family of friends.

2. You may not play the violin,

You may not play the harp,

But everyone can celebrate

No matter who you are.

If you have a face, then you can smile.

If you have eyes that can see

Celebrating comes from inside

The hearts of   you   and   me.

(Sing Chorus)

(Continued)

3. He   gave   us   mountains that climb so high and

He   gave   us   trees to bring shade.

He   gave   us   God's Word to look inside

The hearts of those he made.

He   gave   us   friends that help us thru and

He   gave   us   songs in the night.

He   gave   us clouds when the   sky   is not blue.

He   gave   us the sun to bring light.

(Sing Chorus)

Away in a Manger

VERSION 1

Verse 3 by John Thomas McFarland; Music by James R. Murray

THEME	SCRIPTURE	ENERGY LEVEL
Christmas/Jesus' birth	Isaiah 9:6	Low

Lyrics:

way in a man - ger, no crib for a bed, the
cat - tle are low - ing, the Ba - by a - wakes, the

lit - tle Lord Je - sus laid down his sweet head. The
lit - tle Lord Je - sus, no cry - ing he makes. I

stars in the sky looked down where he lay, the
love thee, Lord Je - sus! Look down from the sky and

lit - tle Lord Je - sus, a - sleep on the hay.
stay by my side un - til morn - ing is nigh.

Away in a Manger

Away in a Manger — VERSION 2

Verse 3 by John Thomas McFarland; Music by James R. Murray

THEME	SCRIPTURE	ENERGY LEVEL
Christmas/Jesus' birth	Isaiah 9:6	Low

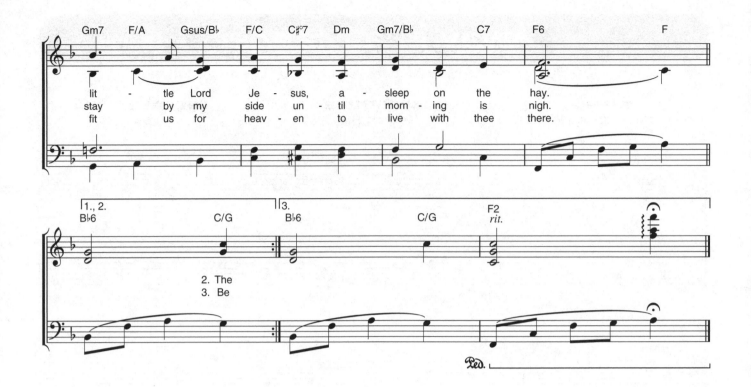

lit - tle Lord Je - sus, a - sleep on the hay.
stay by my side un - til morn - ing is nigh.
fit us for heav - en to live with thee there.

2. The
3. Be

Away in a Manger

Children, Children

Words and Music by Robert C. Evans

THEME	SCRIPTURE	ENERGY LEVEL
God's love	Matthew 18:1-5	Medium

Child - ren, child - ren, come and lis - ten, come and hear ___ of

Je - sus' love. ___ Child - ren, child - ren, come and see ___ him,

come and see ___ how Je - sus loves. ___ Child - ren, child - ren,

come and touch ___ him, come and touch ___ our Bi - ble friend. ___

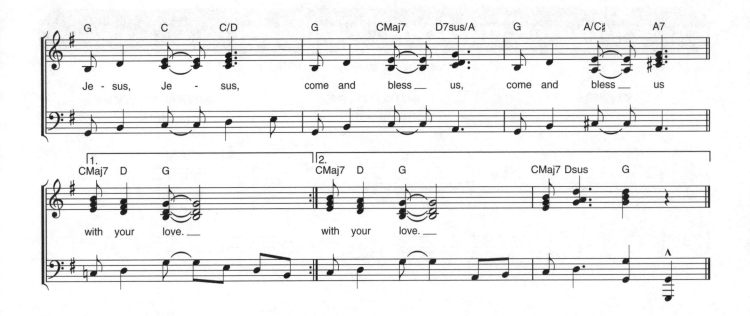

Children, Children

Children,   children,   come   and   listen,

Come   and   hear   of   Jesus'   love.

Children,   children,   come   and   see   him,

Come   and   see   how   Jesus   loves.

Children,   children,   come   and   touch   him,

Come   and   touch   our   Bible   friend.

Jesus,   Jesus,   come   and   bless   us,

Come   and   bless   us   with   your   love.

(Repeat)

Everybody Give Thanks!

Words and Music by Dan McGowan

THEME	**SCRIPTURE**	**ENERGY LEVEL**
Thanksgiving	Psalm 136:1-3	Medium

Copyright © 1994 Dan McGowan. Used by permission.

ACTIONS for EVERYBODY GIVE THANKS!

1. God made the bugs and birds and bees.

God made turtles, toads, and trees.

God made everything we see.

God did this all for you and me!

Chorus:

Everybody give thanks!

Everybody give thanks!

Everybody give thanks to God above

For showering us with his love.

Everybody give thanks!

Everybody give thanks!

Everybody give thanks

For all those blessings from above!

2. God made the ground beneath our feet.

God made all the food we eat.

God made the people that we meet.

God did this all for you and me!

(Sing Chorus)
We thank him every day

For all he sends our way.

And every time we pray,

We say, "We thank you, God!"

(Sing Chorus)

Everybody Give Thanks!

1. God   made   the   bugs   and   birds   and   bees.

God   made   turtles,   toads,   and   trees.

God   made   everything   we   see.

God   did   this   all   for   you   and   me!

Chorus:
Everybody   give   thanks!   Everybody   give   thanks!

Everybody   give   thanks   to   God   above

For   showering   us   with   his   love.

Everybody   give   thanks!   Everybody   give   thanks!

Everybody   give   thanks

For   all   those   blessings   from   above!

(Continued)

Everybody Give Thanks!

2. God made the ground beneath our feet.

God made all the food we eat.

God made the people that we meet.

God did this all for you and me!

(Sing Chorus)

We thank him every day

For all he sends our way.

And every time we pray,

We say, "We thank you, God!"

(Sing Chorus)

Copyright © 1994 Dan McGowan. Used by permission.

He Forgives Me

Words and Music by Mary Rice Hopkins

THEME	SCRIPTURE	ENERGY LEVEL
Forgiveness	1 John 1:9	Low

He Forgives Me

ACTIONS for HE FORGIVES ME

1. Further than anyone can throw,

That's how far his love will go.

Deeper than the deepest sea,

That's how much he forgives me,

Forgives me.

Chorus:
He forgives

(Echo) All my sin.

He forgives

(Echo) Again and again.

He forgives

(Echo) If I ask him

He forgives.

2. More than I can   multiply

And all the   times   I ask Mom   "Why?"

Further than my   eyes   can   see,

That's how much he forgives   me,

Forgives   me!

(Repeat Chorus twice)
3. Whiter than the snow that falls,

And I   know   he   cleans it all.

Higher than the clouds above,

That's how great is   Jesus'   love!

Jesus' love forgives me! Jesus' love forgives me!

Copyright © 1990 Pauline Krystal Music/Big Steps 4 U. All rights reserved. ASCAP

He Forgives Me   45

Down in My Heart

Words and Music by George W. Cooke

THEME	SCRIPTURE	ENERGY LEVEL
Celebration/Joy	1 Peter 1:8	High

1. I have the joy, ____ joy, ____ joy, ____ joy ____ down in my heart– (where?) Down in my heart– (where?) Down in my heart. I have the
2. peace that pass - es un - der - stand - ing down in my heart– (where?) Down in my heart– (where?) Down in my heart. I have the
3. love of Je - sus, love of Je - sus down in my heart– (where?) Down in my heart– (where?) Down in my heart. I have the

1. joy, ____ joy, ____ joy, ____ joy ____ down in my heart– (where?)
2. peace that pass - es un - der - stand - ing
3. love of Je - sus, love of Je - sus

Down in my heart to stay.

2. I have the stay.
3. I have the

1. I have the joy,   joy,   joy,   joy

Down in my heart—where?

Down in my heart—where?

Down in my heart.

I have the joy,   joy,   joy,   joy

Down in my heart—where?

Down in my heart to stay.

2. I have the peace that passes understanding

Down in my heart—where?

Down in my heart—where?

Down in my heart.

I have the peace that passes understanding

Down in my heart—where?

Down in my heart to stay.

3. I have the   love   of   Jesus,   love   of   Jesus

Down in my heart—where?

Down in my heart—where?

Down in my heart.

I have the   love   of   Jesus,   love   of   Jesus

  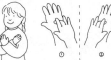

Down in my heart—where?

Down in my heart to stay.

Down in My Heart

The Family

Words and Music by Mark Royce and Barry McGuire

THEME
Body of Christ/The church

SCRIPTURE
1 Corinthians 12:27

ENERGY LEVEL
Medium

The Family

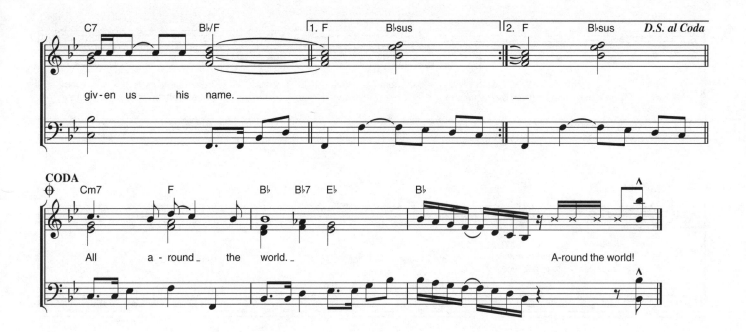

giv-en us ___ his name. ___

CODA

All a - round ___ the world. _

A-round the world!

Go, Tell It on the Mountain

Traditional

THEME	SCRIPTURE	ENERGY LEVEL
Christmas/Jesus' birth	Luke 2:8-21	Medium

Go, Tell It on the Mountain

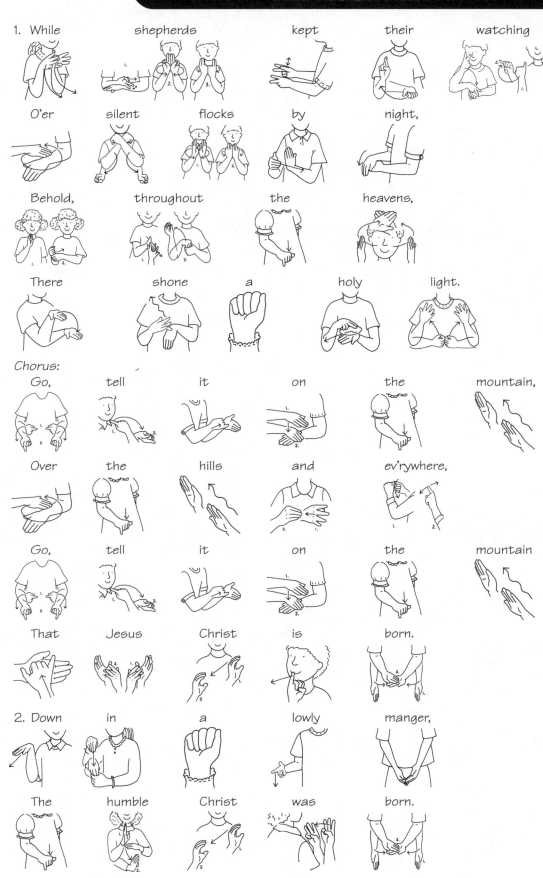

1. While shepherds kept their watching

O'er silent flocks by night,

Behold, throughout the heavens,

There shone a holy light.

Chorus:
Go, tell it on the mountain,

Over the hills and ev'rywhere,

Go, tell it on the mountain

That Jesus Christ is born.

2. Down in a lowly manger,

The humble Christ was born.

(Continued)

And brought us God's salvation

That blessed Christmas morn.

(Sing Chorus)

He's Alive

Words and Music by Jerry Blacklaw

THEME	SCRIPTURE	ENERGY LEVEL
Easter	Luke 24:5-6a	High

God's Got a Plan

Words and Music by Mark Royce and Barry McGuire

THEME	SCRIPTURE	ENERGY LEVEL
God's sovereignty/God's plans for us	Jeremiah 29:11	High

know us now like he knew us then. He wants to
Jesus is the one who paid my debt. And it's the

know us and to love us and to teach us the way. He wants to
same today as it was back then. We can

1. show us his plan and help us learn to obey.

2. follow the world or we can follow him.

God's got a plan work-in' in the world to-day.

God's got a plan work-in' in the world to-day. When the going

gets rough, I'm gonna stick with the plan. When things get tough, I'm gonna follow the Man.

God's Got a Plan

The Holy Books

Words and Music by James Ward

THEME
God's Word

SCRIPTURE
Psalm 119:105

ENERGY LEVEL
Medium

These are ___ the ho-ly ___ books! Tell me the names, ___ and ___ I'll take a sec-ond look! This is ___ his ho-ly ___ Word! Tell this mes-sage 'til all have heard! Gen-e-sis, Ex-o-dus, Le-vit-i-cus, Num-bers, Deu-te-ron-o-my, Josh-u-a, Judg-es, I'll tell you the truth ___ a-bout the book of Ruth. On to

To Coda

Use repeat on D.S. too

First and Sec-ond Sam - uel, First and Sec-ond Kings, First and Sec-ond Chron-i - cles. All those things lead to

Ez - ra, Ne - he - mi - ah, Es - ther, and Job. I wan-na go to heav-en in a right-eous robe sing-in'

Psalms, Pro - verbs, Ec - cle - si - as - tes, Sol - o - mon's Song. And the pro-phets are these: I -

sai - ah, Jer - e - mi - ah, and J's la - ment, E - ze - kiel, then Dan - iel to the li - ons went.

Ho - se - a, Joel, and A - mos'_ tale, O - ba - di - ah, Jo - nah in the bel - ly of the whale.

D.S. al Coda

Mi - cah, Na - hum, and Hab - ak - kuk's cry, Zeph - a - ni - ah, Hag - ga - i, then Zech - a - riah. The

last Old Test - a - ment books re - veal ___ that Mal - a - chi points to a brand new deal!

CODA 1

Mat - thew, Mark, Luke, and John— the sto - ry of Je - sus. And then move on ___ to

Acts and the let - ters of Paul: Ro - mans, First and Sec - ond Cor - in - thi - ans all, Gal -

a - tians, E - phe - sians, Phil - ip - pians, Col - os - sians, and move on ___ to First and Se - cond Thes - sa - lon - i - ans,

He Can Do

Words and Music by Mary Rice Hopkins

THEME
God's power

SCRIPTURE
Philippians 4:13

ENERGY LEVEL
Medium

He Can Do

God's Not Dead

Author Unknown

THEME	SCRIPTURE	ENERGY LEVEL
Easter	1 Timothy 4:10	High

Chorus:

God's   not   dead,   (No!)

He is   alive.

God's   not   dead,   (No!)

He is   alive.

God's   not   dead,   (No!)

He is   alive.

I   know   he's living in   me.

I   see   him in my hands.

I   see   him in my   feet.

I   see   him in the air.

I   see   him   ev'rywhere.

I   see   him at the   church.

I   see   him on the street,

And I   know   he's living in   me.

No,   no,   no,   no,   no,   no,   no . . .

(Sing Chorus)

He Never Sleeps

Author Unknown

THEME
God's watchful
presence/Scripture song

SCRIPTURE
Psalm 121:3-4

ENERGY LEVEL
Low

He nev-er sleeps; he nev-er slum-bers. He watch-es me both night and day. He nev-er sleeps; he nev-er slum-bers. He keeps me safe a-long the

He   never   sleeps;

He   never   slumbers.

He   watches   me

Both night and   day.

He   never   sleeps;

He   never   slumbers.

He keeps   me   safe

Along the way.

I don't have to   worry;

My soul's in his   care.

I don't have to   worry

'Cause he's always there.

I   know   that he's   watching

Wherever I go.

I   know   that he's   watching

'Cause he told me so.

(Repeat)

I Will Call Upon the Lord

Words and Music by Michael O'Shields

THEME	SCRIPTURE	ENERGY LEVEL
Prayer/Scripture song	Psalm 18:3; Matthew 6:9-13	Medium

I Will Call Upon the Lord

I Am a Promise

Words and Music by William J. and Gloria Gaither

THEME	SCRIPTURE	ENERGY LEVEL
God's sovereignty/God's plans for us/Self-esteem	Ephesians 2:10	Medium

an - y - thing God wants me   to   be. ___   I   am   a ___

I Am a Promise

I am a promise, I am a possibility,

I am a promise with a capital P,

I am a great big bundle of potentiality.

And I am learnin' to hear

God's voice,

And I am tryin' to make the

right choices.

I'm a promise to be anything God

wants me to be.

(Repeat)

Hip, Hip, Hooray

Words and Music by Mary Rice Hopkins

THEME
Creation

SCRIPTURE
Genesis 2:19

ENERGY LEVEL
High

1. In the be - gin - ning, God made the sea and the for - est filled with trees. He made the moun - tains up so high. On the ver - y top, he placed the sky.
2. (God's) fin - ger - prints are ev - 'ry - where just to show how much he cares. In be - tween he had loads of fun, he made a hip - po who weighs a ton.
3. (Cre) - a - tion sings of his praise, the spar - row and the tin - y babe. We can sing and say well done, but some things he just made for fun.

Hip, hip, hip, hip - po - pot - a - mus, hip, hip, hoo - ray, God made all of us.

ACTIONS for HIP, HIP, HOORAY

1. In the beginning,   God   made the sea

And the forest filled with   trees.

He made the   mountains   up   so high.

On the very   top,   he placed the   sky.

Chorus:
Hip, hip, hip, hippopotamus,

Hip, hip, hooray,   God   made all of us.

Hip, hip, hip, hippopotamus,

Hip, hip, hooray, he made us.

2. *God's   fingerprints   are   ev'rywhere*

Just to show how much he   cares.

In between he had loads of   fun,

He made a hippo who weighs a ton.

(Sing Chorus)
3. Creation sings of his   praise,

The sparrow and the tiny   babe.

We can sing and say well done,

But some things he just made for   fun.

(Sing Chorus)

Made us!

Hip, Hip, Hooray

It's a Miracle

Words and Music by William J. and Gloria Gaither

THEME	SCRIPTURE	ENERGY LEVEL
Creation/God's sovereignty/ God's plans for us/God's power	Psalm 8:3	Medium

It's a Miracle

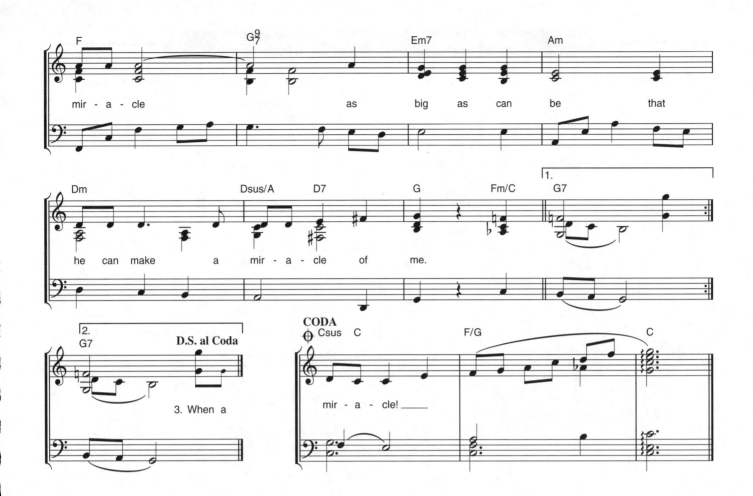

1. What drives the stars without making a sound?

Why don't they crash when they're spinning around?

What holds me up when the world's upside down?

I know—it's a miracle.

Who tells the ocean where to stop on the sand?

What keeps the water back from drowning the land?

Who makes the rules? I don't understand.

I know—it's a miracle!

Chorus:
   It's a miracle just to know

God is with me wherever I go.

It's a miracle as big as can be

That he can make a miracle of me.

2. Who shows the birds how to make a good nest?

How can the geese fly so far without rest?

Why do the ducks go south and not west?

I know—it's a miracle.

What makes a brown seed so tiny and dry

Burst into green and grow up so high?

And shoot out the blossoms of red by and by?

I know—it's a miracle!

(Sing Chorus)

(Continued)

It's a Miracle

ACTIONS for IT'S A MIRACLE

3. When a spring makes a brook and a brook makes a stream,

The stream makes the   river   water fresh as can be.

Who puts the   salt   in when it gets to the sea?

I   know—it's a   miracle.

There are thousands of people in cities I   see.

The   world   must be crowded as crowded can be.

But God knows my name and he cares about me!

I   know—it's a   miracle!

Copyright © 1975, 1995 William J. Gaither. All rights reserved. International copyright secured.

It's a Miracle

I Will Praise You

Words and Music by Mark Royce and Barry McGuire

THEME	SCRIPTURE	ENERGY LEVEL
Praising God	Psalm 5	Medium

CODA

praise. _____ You stand be-side me. Your hand will guide me. You fill my heart with

praise. _____ You fill my heart with praise. _____

You fill my heart with praise. Hey!

Early every morning

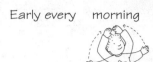

When the sun begins to shine

And I open up my eyes,

I will praise you.

(Repeat)
All day long

I give my life to you.

In everything I do,

I will praise you.

(Repeat)
You stand beside me.

Your hand will guide me.

You fill my heart with praise.

(Repeat)
(Repeat Verses)
You fill my heart with praise.

You fill my heart with praise.

Hey!

He's Got the Whole World in His Hands

Traditional

THEME	SCRIPTURE	ENERGY LEVEL
God's watchful presence	Psalm 50:10-12	Low

1. He's got the whole   world   in his hands,

He's got the whole   world   in his hands,

He's got the whole   world   in his hands,

He's got the whole   world   in his hands.

Additional Verses:

2. He's got the   wind   and the   rain . . .

3. He's got the little bitty   babies . . .

4. He's got   you   and   me,   brother . . .

5. He's got   you   and   me,   sister . . .

6. He's got   ev'rybody   here . . .

Ho-Ho-Ho-Hosanna

Author Unknown

THEME	SCRIPTURE	ENERGY LEVEL
Celebration/Joy/Easter	Matthew 21:9-11	High

Ho-ho-ho-hosanna!

Ha-ha-hallelujah!

He He He He   saved   me.

I've got the   joy   of the   Lord!

(Repeat twice)

He Is the King of Kings

Words and Music by Virgil Meares

THEME	SCRIPTURE	ENERGY LEVEL
Jesus, our King	Philippians 2:5-11	Medium

He is the King of kings. He is the
Lord of lords. His name is Je - sus, Je - sus,
Je - sus, Je - sus. O... he is the King. He is the King.

His Banner Over Me Is Love

Words and Music by Alfred B. Smith

THEME	SCRIPTURE	ENERGY LEVEL
God's love/Scripture song	Song of Solomon 2:4	Medium

ban - ner   o - ver   me   is   love.

ACTIONS for HIS BANNER OVER ME IS LOVE

1. I'm my beloved's and he is mine.

His   banner   over   me   is   love.

I'm my beloved's and he is mine.

His   banner   over   me   is   love.

I'm my beloved's and he is mine.

His   banner   over   me   is   love.

His   banner   over   me   is   love.

Additional Verses:

2. Jesus   is the   Rock   of my salvation . . .

3. The one way to   peace   is the   power

of the   Cross . . .

4. He is the Vine and we are the branches . . .

5. I'm feasting at his   banqueting   table . . .

6. He   lifts us up   to heavenly places . . .

Ha-La-La-La*

Words and Music by David Graham

THEME	SCRIPTURE	ENERGY LEVEL
Celebration/Joy	Revelation 19:6	High

Ha-La-La-La

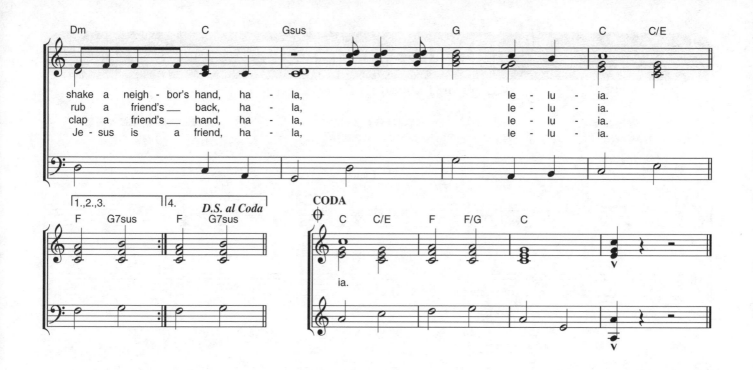

shake a neigh-bor's hand, ha - la, le - lu - ia.
rub a friend's ___ back, ha - la, le - lu - ia.
clap a friend's ___ hand, ha - la, le - lu - ia.
Je - sus is a friend, ha - la, le - lu - ia.

1.,2.,3.   4.   *D.S. al Coda*   **CODA**
F   G7sus   F   G7sus   C   C/E   F   F/G   C

ia.

Ha-La-La-La

This Is the Day

Words and Music by Les Garrett

THEME
Celebration/Joy/
Creation/Scripture song

SCRIPTURE
Psalm 118:24

ENERGY LEVEL
High

The Butterfly Song (If I Were a Butterfly)

Words and Music by Brian Howard

THEME
Made in God's image

SCRIPTURE
Genesis 1:28

ENERGY LEVEL
Medium

1. If I were a   butterfly,

I'd thank you,   Lord, for   giving   me wings.

And if I were a   robin   in a   tree,

I'd thank you,   Lord,   that I could sing.

And if I were a   fish   in the sea,

I'd wiggle my tail,

And I'd giggle with glee.

But I just thank   you,   Father,   for makin'

me   "me."

Chorus:
  'Cause you   gave   me a   heart,

and you   gave   me a smile,

You   gave   me   Jesus,   and

you   made   me   your child.

And I just thank   you,   Father,   for making

me   "me."

2. If I were an   elephant,

I'd thank   you,   Lord,   by raising my   trunk.

And if I were a   kangaroo,

I'd just hop right up to   you.

And if I were an   octopus,

(Continued)

ACTIONS for THE BUTTERFLY SONG
(IF I WERE A BUTTERFLY)

I'd thank you, Lord, for my good looks.

But I just thank you, Father, for making

me "me."

(Sing Chorus)

3. If I were a wiggly worm,

I'd thank you, Lord, that I could squirm.

And if I were a crocodile,

I'd thank you, Lord, for my big smile.

And if I were a fuzzy wuzzy bear,

I'd thank you, Lord, for my fuzzy wuzzy hair.

But I just thank you, Father, for making

me "me."

(Sing Chorus)

The Butterfly Song (If I Were a Butterfly)

Kids of the Kingdom

Words and Music by Ralph Torres

THEME	SCRIPTURE	ENERGY LEVEL
Body of Christ/The church/ God's family/Self-esteem	Ecclesiastes 4:9-12	Medium

Kids of the Kingdom

I Will Dwell in the House of the Lord

Words and Music by Ron Stinnett

THEME	SCRIPTURE	ENERGY LEVEL
God's watchful presence/Jesus, our Good Shepherd/Scripture song	Psalm 23	Medium

I Will Dwell in the House of the Lord

1. The   Lord   is   my   shepherd,   I   shall   not   want,

Shall   not   want,   oh,   I   shall   not   want.

The   Lord   is   my   shepherd,   I   shall   not   want

All   the   days   of   my   life.

Chorus:

And   I   will   dwell   in   the   house

of   the   Lord,

House   of   the   Lord,   in   the   house

of   the   Lord.

I   will   dwell   in   the   house   of   the   Lord

Now   and   forevermore.

(Continued)

2. Thy rod and thy staff, they comfort me,

Comfort me, oh, they comfort me.

Thy rod and thy staff, they comfort me

All the days of my life.

(Sing Chorus)

3. Goodness and mercy shall follow me,

Follow me, they shall follow me.

Goodness and mercy shall follow me

All the days of my life.

(Sing Chorus)

(Repeat Verse 1 and Chorus)

Jesus Is the Rock

Words and Music by Tony Congi

THEME	SCRIPTURE	ENERGY LEVEL
Jesus, our Cornerstone	Mark 12:10-11	High

Chorus:
Well, my Jesus is a rock, and he

rolls my blues away! Bop she-bop, she-bop, wooo!

Jesus is a rock, and he rolls my

blues away! Bop she-bop, she-bop, wooo!

Jesus is a rock, and he rolls my blues away!

When you wake up in the mornin', and the sky ain't

bright and blue. Bop she-bop, she-bop, wooo!

When you wake up in the mornin', and the big

world's after you. Bop she-bop, she-bop, wooo!

When you wake up in the mornin',

Jesus' gonna pull you through!

(Sing Chorus)
When you're out on the streets,

and you're really feelin' down and low,

When you're out on the streets,

and there's really no place to go,

When you're out on the streets,

well, Jesus' gonna save your soul!

(Sing Chorus)
When you look in a mirror,

and your face causes it to crack,

When you're through with your day

(Continued)

and you feel like you've been attacked,

Well,   Jesus'   gonna   love   you,   baby,

now that's a   fact!

Well, my   Jesus   is a   rock,   and he

rolls my blues   away!   Bop she-bop, she-bop, wooo!

Jesus   is a   rock,   and he rolls my

blues   away!   Bop she-bop, she-bop, wooo!

Jesus   is a   rock,   and he rolls my blues,

Jesus   is a   rock,   and he rolls my blues,

Jesus   is a   rock,   and he rolls my blues   away!

I Believe in Jesus

Words and Music by Marc Nelson

THEME	SCRIPTURE	ENERGY LEVEL
Faith	1 Thessalonians 4:14	Low

All: I believe in Jesus.

I believe he is the Son of God.

I believe he died and rose again.

I believe he paid for us all.

Group 1: I believe he's here now,

Group 2: I believe he is here,

All: Standing in our midst.

Group 1: Here with the power to heal now,

Group 2: With the power to heal,

All: And the grace to forgive.

King of Kings

Sophie Conty and Nomi Yah
Ancient Hebrew Folk Song

THEME	SCRIPTURE	ENERGY LEVEL
Jesus, our King/Scripture song	Hebrews 2:9	Medium

Masterpiece

Words and Music by Dan McGowan

THEME	SCRIPTURE	ENERGY LEVEL
Made in God's image	Psalm 139:13	Medium

1. Up in hea-ven ma-ny years a-go, God was mak-ing shoul-ders, knees, and toes. He put them all to-geth-er and paint-ed them with love, and he made me what my mom is thank-ful of.

2. He cre-a-ted me the way I look us-ing all the piec-es that he took. I'm so glad he made me the way I am to-day and that he'll nev-er throw the piec-es a-way.

Like a mas-ter paint-er, God made me art! Like a mas-ter think-er, God made me smart! Like a

I'm Gonna Sing, Sing, Sing

Authors Unknown

THEME	SCRIPTURE	ENERGY LEVEL
Praising God	Psalm 149:1	High

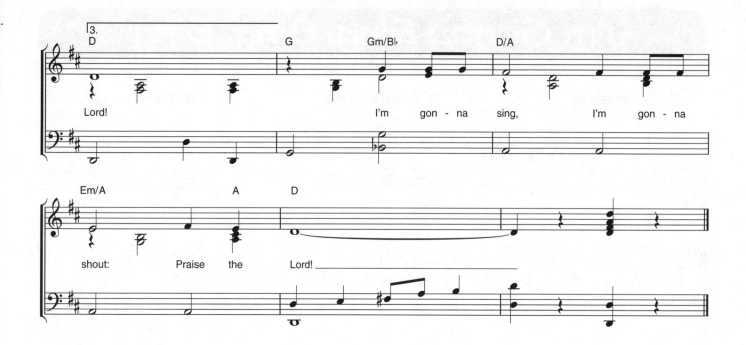

Lord!   I'm gon - na sing,   I'm gon - na

shout: Praise   the   Lord! _____

         I'm Gonna Sing, Sing, Sing

Power of the Lord

Words and Music by Dan McGowan

THEME	SCRIPTURE	ENERGY LEVEL
God's power	Ephesians 1:19-20	Medium

Power of the Lord

ACTIONS for POWER OF THE LORD

Chorus:
I've got the mighty power of the Lord inside me—

Pow, pow, power of the Lord!

I've got the holy power of the Lord inside me—

Pow, pow, power of the Lord!

It doesn't matter what others do.

It doesn't matter what others say.

It only matters that God is in my heart,

And he's promised he will never go away!

(Sing Chorus)
No need to worry, no need to fear,

No need to wonder if the Lord is here.

My God is with me; I know he's by my side,

And because of that I never need to hide!

(Sing Chorus)
When someone's trying to make you mad,

When someone's trying to make you blue,

No need to worry, just remind yourself

That the Lord is living right inside of you!

He's right inside of you.

(Sing Chorus)
I've got the pow, pow, power of the Lord,

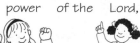 

I've got the pow, pow, power of the Lord!

Ye-haw!

Copyright © 1994 Dan McGowan. Used by permission.

Power of the Lord

Psalm 139:14

THEME
Creation/Made in God's
image/Scripture song

SCRIPTURE
Psalm 139:14

ENERGY LEVEL
Medium

Psalm 139:14

Psalm   one   hundred   thirty-nine,   verse   fourteen

| I | am | fearfully | and | wonderfully | made. |

| I | praise | you | because, |

| I | praise | you | because |

| I | am | fearfully | and | wonderfully | made. |

| I | praise | you | because, |

| I | praise | you | because |

| I | am | fearfully | and | wonderfully | made. |

(Repeat)

| Your | works | are | wonderful, | wonderful. | I | know |

| Your | works | are | wonderful. | I | know | full | well. |

(Continued)

I   praise   you   because,

I   praise   you   because

I   am   fearfully   and   wonderfully   made.

Psalm   one   hundred   thirty-nine   fourteen.

You're Something Special

Words and Music by William J. and Gloria Gaither

THEME	SCRIPTURE	ENERGY LEVEL
God's sovereignty/God's plan for us/Self-esteem	Matthew 10:30	Low

Chorus

I'm some-thing spe-cial— I'm the on - ly one of my kind. _____ God gave me a bod - y and a bright, health - y mind. He had a spe-cial pur-pose that he want - ed me to find, _____ so he made me some-thing spe-cial— I'm the on - ly one of my kind.

1. I
2. My

First time D.S.
2nd time D.S. al Coda ⊕

*That's why

*Lyric for 2nd verse only

You're Something Special

Let Everybody Praise the Lord

Words and Music by Roger Thrower

THEME	SCRIPTURE	ENERGY LEVEL
Praising God	Psalm 150:6	High

Let Everybody Praise the Lord

ACTIONS for LET EVERYBODY PRAISE THE LORD

Chorus:

Let everybody breathin' praise the Lord. *(Praise the Lord!)*

Let everybody breathin' praise the Lord. *(Praise the Lord!)*

Join in creation's choir and lift his praises higher—

Praise the Lord, praise the Lord, praise the Lord.

1. Arise with the rooster and sing. *(Cock-a-doodle-doo!)*

Join the cows in a worship offering. *(Moo!)*

Quack out praises *(quack, quack, quack, quack)*

With the duck. *(Quack, quack, quack, quack!)*

Give thanks with the chickens,

Cluck, cluck, cluck! *(Bok, bok, bok, bok!)*

(Sing Chorus)

2. Join the horses and dance before the Lord. *(Neigh!)*

Stomp your feet with the sheep and praise him

more. *(Baa!)*

Bark your praises *(woof, woof, woof, woof)*

With the dog. *(Woof, woof, woof, woof!)*

Oink out your thanksgiving with the hogs!

(Snort, snort!)

(Sing Chorus)

Praise the Lord, praise the Lord, praise the Lord!

Let Everybody Praise the Lord

Lord, Put a Smile, Smile, Smile on My Face

Words and Music by Rod S. Pringle

THEME	SCRIPTURE	ENERGY LEVEL
Celebration/Joy	Proverbs 17:22	Medium

Lord, Put a Smile, Smile, Smile on My Face

ACTIONS for LORD, PUT A SMILE, SMILE, SMILE ON MY FACE

Lord,   put a   smile, smile, smile   on my   face—

Put a   smile, smile, smile   on my   face.

Lord, when things are going bad, I'm feeling kind of sad,

Put a   smile, smile, smile   on my   face.

Lord,   put a   song,   song,   song   in my   heart—

Put a   song,   song,   song   in my   heart.

Lord, when things are going bad, I'm feeling kind of sad,

Put a   song,   song,   song   in my   heart.

Lord, put a prayer,   prayer,   prayer on my   tongue—

Put a   prayer,   prayer,   prayer   on my   tongue.

Lord, when things are going bad, I'm feeling kind of sad,

Put a   prayer,   prayer,   prayer   on my   tongue.

Lord, put a   smile, smile, smile   on my   face.

Put a   song,   song,   song   in my   heart.

Lord, when things are going bad, I'm feeling kind of sad,

Put a   prayer,   prayer,   prayer   on my   tongue.

Lord,   put a   smile,   song,   prayer   in my life.

Lord, Put a Smile, Smile, Smile on My Face

Rejoice in the Lord Always

Traditional

THEME	SCRIPTURE	ENERGY LEVEL
Celebration/Joy/ Scripture song	Philippians 4:4	Medium

Rejoice   in   the   Lord   always,

Again   I   say,   rejoice!

Rejoice   in   the   Lord   always,

Again   I   say,   rejoice!

Rejoice,   rejoice,

Again   I   say,   rejoice!

Rejoice,   rejoice,

Again   I   say,   rejoice!

(Repeat Verses)

Rejoice   in   the   Lord   always,

Again   I   say,   rejoice!   Rejoice!

Rejoice in the Lord Always

Arky, Arky

Author Unknown

THEME	SCRIPTURE	ENERGY LEVEL
Praising God/Bible story	Genesis 6:5-22	High

ACTIONS for ARKY, ARKY

1. The Lord told Noah, there's gonna be a floody,

   floody,

   Lord   told Noah, there's gonna be a   floody,

   floody.

   Get those animals out of the muddy, muddy,

   Children of the   Lord.

2. The Lord told Noah to build him an arky, arky,

   Lord   told Noah to   build   him an arky, arky.

   Build   it out of gopher barky, barky,

   Children of the   Lord.

Chorus:
So rise and shine

And   give   God   the glory, glory,

Rise and shine

And   give   God   the glory, glory.

Rise and shine

And   give   God   the glory, glory,

Children of the   Lord.

3. The animals, the animals, they came in by
   twosies,   twosies,

   Animals, the animals, they came in by   twosies,

   twosies,

(Continued)

Arky, Arky

Elephants and kangaroosies, roosies,

Children of the Lord!

4. It rained and poured for forty daysies, daysies,

4 TIMES

Rained and poured for forty daysies, daysies,

4 TIMES

Almost drove those animals crazies, crazies,

Children of the Lord!

(Repeat Chorus)

5. The sun came up and dried up the landy, landy,

(Look, there's the sun!) It dried up the landy, landy,

Everything was fine and dandy, dandy,

Children of the Lord!

(Repeat Chorus)

The Body Song

Words and Music by Ann Wamberg

THEME	SCRIPTURE	ENERGY LEVEL
Body of Christ/The church	1 Corinthians 12:20	High

Chorus:
We are the body of Christ.

Oh, the church is the body of Christ.

Everybody is important

And has a job, it's true.

Without each part what would we do?

'Cause some are hands (clap, clap),

Some are feet (stomp, stomp, stomp),

Some are noses (ahchoo!),

Some are ears (Listen up!),

Some are eyes (Hey, look!),

Some are mouths (Good News!),

Some are arms (hug, hug),

Some are hearts, I love you.

(Repeat All)

(Repeat Chorus)

Oh, without each part what would we do?

Oh, without each part what would we do?

Sing (If You Wanna Be Happy)

Words and Music by Caye Cook

THEME	SCRIPTURE	ENERGY LEVEL
Celebration/Joy/ Praising God	Ephesians 5:19-20	Medium

ACTIONS for SING
(IF YOU WANNA BE HAPPY)

1. Sing, if you wanna be happy!

Sing, if you wanna give praise!

Sing while holding this note real long . . .

Sing praise to God all day long. Ba-da, dum, dum.

2. Clap, if you wanna be happy!

Clap, if you wanna give praise!

Clap while holding this note real long . . .

Sing praise to God all day long. Ba-da, dum, dum.

3. Jump, if you wanna be happy!

Jump, if you wanna give praise!

Jump while holding this note real long . . .

Sing praise to God all day long. Ba-da, dum, dum.

4. Gargle, if you wanna be happy!

Gargle, if you wanna give praise!

Gargle while holding this note real long . . .

Sing praise to God all day long. Ba-da, dum, dum.

5. Pout, if you don't wanna be happy.

Pout, if you don't wanna give praise.

Pout while holding this note real long . . .

Be miserable all day long. But why don't you . . .

(Repeat Verse 1)

Sing (If You Wanna Be Happy)

Morning Star

Words and Music by Mary Rice Hopkins

THEME
Made in God's image

SCRIPTURE
Genesis 1:27

ENERGY LEVEL
Low

1. Like a pot-ter who works the clay, God made me in his own special way. A morn-ing star to shine through the day, and I'll be like my Fa-ther, I'll show-'em the love he made. Like a

2. God could have made me like a puppet on a string. But I would-n't have choi-ces and I would-n't have wings. But I'm free to fly and soar with the wind, and be all that he made me, a bright and mor-ning star.

morn-ing, morn-ing star. Like a

CODA

3. Like a pot - ter who works the clay,

God made me in his own spe - cial way, a morn - ing star to

shine through the day. And I'll be like my Fa - ther, a bright and mor - ning star.

O, Clap Your Hands

Words and Music by Bob Stromberg

THEME	**SCRIPTURE**	**ENERGY LEVEL**
Praising God	Psalm 47:1	High

O, clap your hands,

O, stomp your feet,

Slap on your knees,

Get off your seat,

And sing allelu, allelu!

Now shout amen, amen!

Allelu, allelu, amen!

(Repeat)

We Say Shalom

Words and Music by Mark Royce and Barry McGuire

THEME	SCRIPTURE	ENERGY LEVEL
Cultural diversity/Peace	John 14:27	Medium

We Say Shalom

We say shalom,

We say shalom,

We say shalom,

When we meet each other every   day.

We say shalom

When we get together just to play.

We say shalom

So the peace of   God   will lead the way.

We say shalom.

We say shalom.

We say shalom to say   hello,

Shalom to say   goodbye.

Shalom—may   you   live in   peace.

We say shalom to say   hello,

Shalom to say   goodbye.

Shalom—may   you   live in   peace.

(Repeat All)

We say shalom,

We say shalom,

We say shalom—may   you   live in   peace.

Seek Ye First

Words and Music by Karen Lafferty

THEME	SCRIPTURE	ENERGY LEVEL
Following God/Prayer/ Scripture song	Matthew 6:33; 7:7	Low

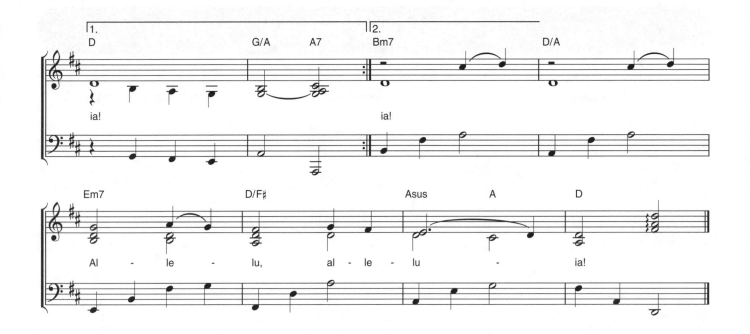

Seek Ye First

What a Mighty God We Serve

Author Unknown

THEME	SCRIPTURE	ENERGY LEVEL
God's power	Luke 1:37	Medium

What a might - y God we serve,

what a might - y God we serve.

An - gels bow be - fore ___ him, ___ Heaven and earth a - dore ___ him. ___

What a might - y God we serve. _____

Sing Unto the Lord

Author Unknown

THEME	SCRIPTURE	ENERGY LEVEL
Praising God	Psalm 96:1-2	High

Chorus:

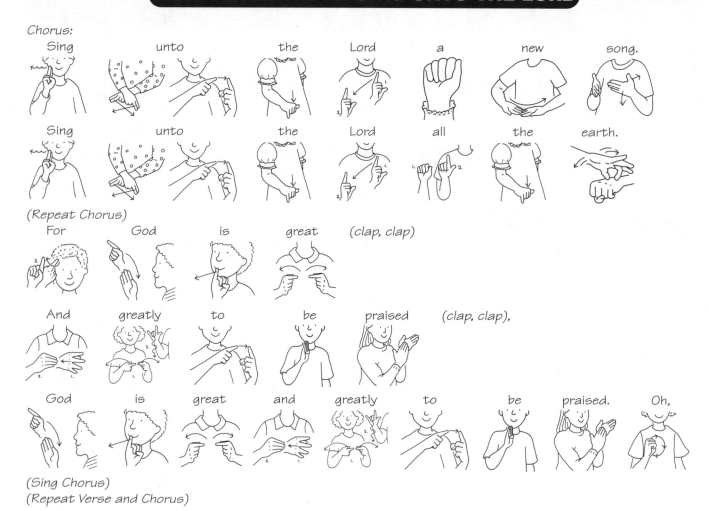

Sing   unto   the   Lord   a   new   song.

Sing   unto   the   Lord   all   the   earth.

(Repeat Chorus)

For   God   is   great   *(clap, clap)*

And   greatly   to   be   praised   *(clap, clap),*

God   is   great   and   greatly   to   be   praised.   Oh,

(Sing Chorus)
(Repeat Verse and Chorus)

Victory Chant

Words and Music by Joseph Vogels

THEME	SCRIPTURE	ENERGY LEVEL
Jesus, our King	Revelation 19:6	Medium

The Wise Man and the Foolish Man

Author Unknown

THEME	SCRIPTURE	ENERGY LEVEL
Faith/Bible story/ Scripture song	Matthew 7:24-27	Medium

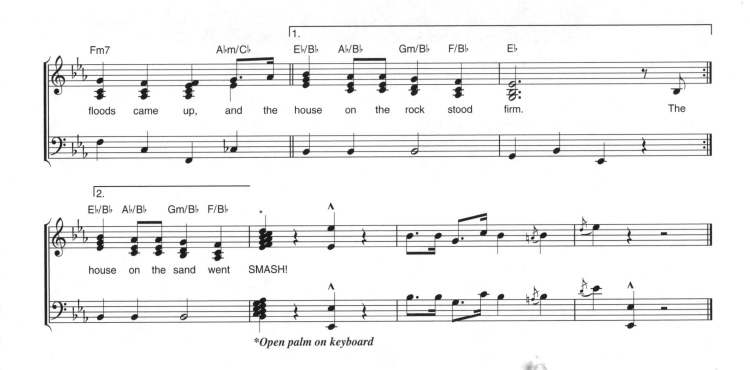

*Open palm on keyboard

The wise man   built   his house upon the   rock,

The wise man   built   his house upon the   rock,

The wise man   built   his house upon the   rock,

And the   rains   came tumblin'   down.

The   rains   came   down   and the   floods   came   up,

The   rains   came   down   and the   floods   came   up,

The   rains   came   down   and the   floods   came   up,

And the house on the   rock   stood firm.

The foolish man   built   his house upon the   sand,

The foolish man   built   his house upon the   sand,

The foolish man   built   his house upon the   sand,

And the   rains   came tumblin'   down.

The   rains   came   down   and the   floods   came   up,

The   rains   came   down   and the   floods   came   up,

The   rains   came   down   and the   floods   came   up,

And the house on the   sand   went SMASH!

You Are My Shepherd

Words and Music by Mary Rice Hopkins and Denny Bouchard

THEME	SCRIPTURE	ENERGY LEVEL
Jesus, our Good Shepherd	John 10:11	Low

You Are My Shepherd

You Are My Shepherd

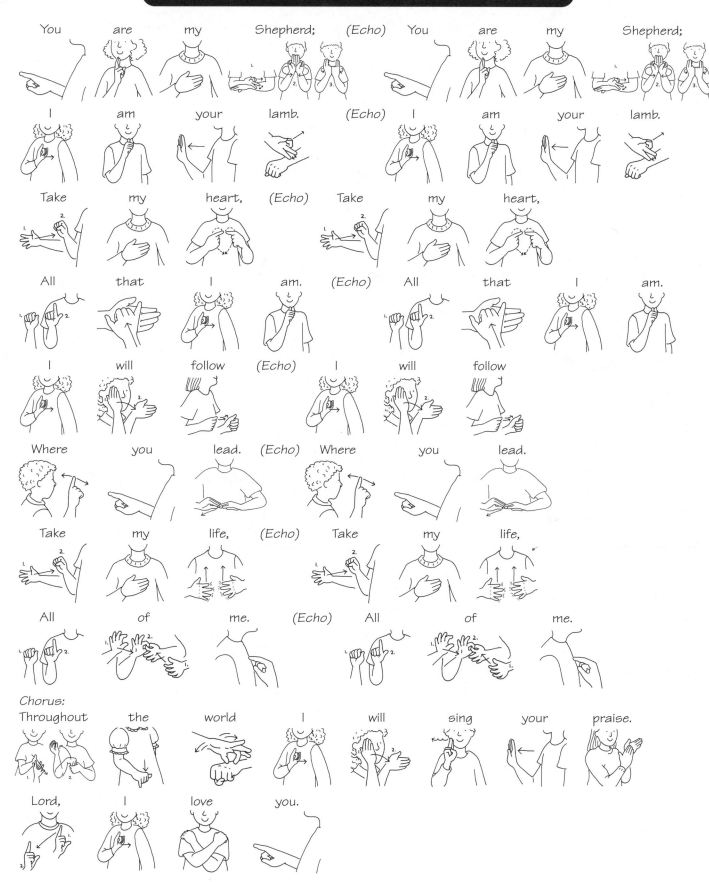

You	are	my	Shepherd;	(Echo)	You	are	my	Shepherd;
I	am	your	lamb.	(Echo)	I	am	your	lamb.
Take	my	heart,	(Echo)	Take	my	heart,
All	that	I	am.	(Echo)	All	that	I	am.
I	will	follow	(Echo)	I	will	follow
Where	you	lead.	(Echo)	Where	you	lead.
Take	my	life,	(Echo)	Take	my	life,
All	of	me.	(Echo)	All	of	me.

Chorus:
| Throughout | the | world | I | will | sing | your | praise. |
| Lord, | I | love | you. |

(Continued)

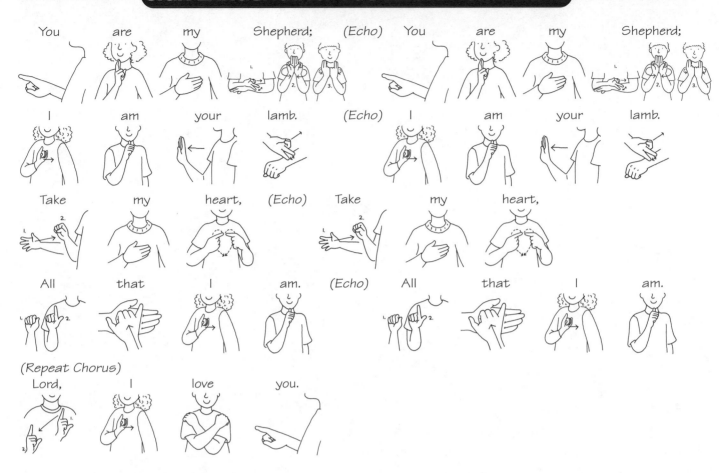

You   are   my   Shepherd;   (Echo)   You   are   my   Shepherd;

I   am   your   lamb.   (Echo)   I   am   your   lamb.

Take   my   heart,   (Echo)   Take   my   heart,

All   that   I   am.   (Echo)   All   that   I   am.

(Repeat Chorus)

Lord,   I   love   you.

Stand Up and Sing

Words and Music by Bob and Barbara Dawson

THEME	SCRIPTURE	ENERGY LEVEL
Praising God	1 Chronicles 16:9	High

Stand Up and Sing

Stand   up,   sit   down,

Praise   the name of   Jesus.

Stand   up,   sit   down,

He's my risen   Lord.

Stand   up,   sit   down,

Praise   the name of   Jesus.

Stand   up,   sit   down,

His   joy   is my reward.

Sing hallelujah,

Come   and sing it out.

Tell him   you   love   him,

Praise   him with a shout!

Shout hallelujah!

Praise   to the   King.

Lift   your hands to   praise   him,

Rejoice and sing.

Stand   up,   sit   down,

Praise   the name of   Jesus.

Stand   up,   sit   down,

He's my risen   Lord.

(Continued)

Stand   up,   sit   down,

Praise   the name of   Jesus.

Stand   up,   sit   down,

His   joy   is my reward.

His   joy   is my reward.

Sing a Song of Praise

Words and Music by Keith Currie

THEME	SCRIPTURE	ENERGY LEVEL
Praising God	James 5:13b	Medium

Sing a Song of Praise

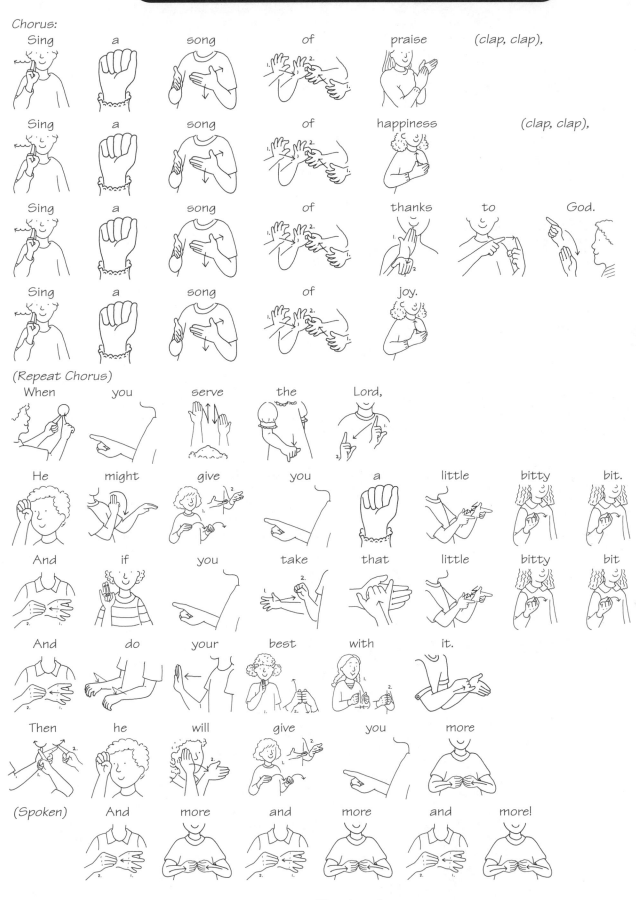

Chorus:

Sing	a	song	of	praise	(clap, clap),

Sing	a	song	of	happiness	(clap, clap),

Sing	a	song	of	thanks	to	God.

Sing	a	song	of	joy.

(Repeat Chorus)

When	you	serve	the	Lord,

He	might	give	you	a	little	bitty	bit.

And	if	you	take	that	little	bitty	bit

And	do	your	best	with	it.

Then	he	will	give	you	more

(Spoken)	And	more	and	more	and	more!

(Continued)

SIGN LANGUAGE for SING A SONG OF PRAISE

And   you   will   hear   him   say,

Come   and   join   my   celebration.

(Sing Chorus)
Sing   a   song   of   joy.

We're   going   to   sing   a

song   of   joy.

Be True

Words and Music by Ann Wamberg

THEME	SCRIPTURE	ENERGY LEVEL
God sees the heart	1 Samuel 16:7b	Medium

Title Index

Scripture Index

Theme Index

Energy Level Index

Action Songs Index

Sign Language Songs Index

Lyrics Big Book for Group Singing

Lyrics Big Book for More Group Singing

Cassette/Compact Disc

Volume 1
1. Come, Meet Jesus!
2. Lord, I Lift Your Name on High
3. Down in Bethlehem
4. The B-I-B-L-E
5. 1 Thessalonians 4:17
6. Awesome God
7. Cares Chorus
8. The Best Gift
9. Celebration Song
10. Away in a Manger
11. Children, Children
12. Everybody Give Thanks!
13. He Forgives Me
14. Down in My Heart
15. The Family
16. Go, Tell It on the Mountain

Volume 2
1. He's Alive
2. God's Got a Plan
3. The Holy Books
4. He Can Do
5. God's Not Dead
6. He Never Sleeps
7. I Will Call Upon the Lord
8. I Am a Promise
9. Hip, Hip, Hooray
10. It's a Miracle
11. I Will Praise You
12. He's Got the Whole World in His Hands
13. Ho-Ho-Ho-Hosanna
14. He Is the King of Kings
15. His Banner Over Me Is Love

Volume 3
1. Ha-La-La-La
2. This Is the Day
3. The Butterfly Song (If I Were a Butterfly)
4. Kids of the Kingdom
5. I Will Dwell in the House of the Lord
6. Jesus Is the Rock
7. I Believe in Jesus
8. King of Kings
9. Masterpiece
10. I'm Gonna Sing, Sing, Sing
11. Power of the Lord
12. Psalm 139:14
13. You're Something Special
14. Let Everybody Praise the Lord
15. Lord, Put a Smile, Smile, Smile on My Face
16. Rejoice in the Lord Always

Volume 4
1. Arky, Arky
2. The Body Song
3. Sing (If You Wanna Be Happy)
4. Morning Star
5. O, Clap Your Hands
6. We Say Shalom
7. Seek Ye First
8. What a Mighty God We Serve
9. Sing Unto the Lord
10. Victory Chant
11. The Wise Man and the Foolish Man
12. You Are My Shepherd
13. Stand Up and Sing
14. Sing a Song of Praise
15. Be True